The Invisible Seed
by Dienabou Diallo

The Invisible Seed

Copyright © 2015 by Dienabou Diallo

All rights reserved. No part of this publication may be reproduced, distributed, or transmitted in any form or by any means, including photocopying, recording, or other electronic or mechanical methods, without the prior written permission of the publisher or author, except in the case of brief quotations embodied in critical reviews and certain other noncommercial uses permitted by copyright law. For permission requests, email the author at (dsdiena@gmail.com).

The content of this book is for general instruction only. Each person's physical, emotional, and spiritual condition is unique. The instruction in this book is not intended to replace or interrupt the reader's relationship with a physician or other professionals. Please consult your doctor for matters pertaining to your specific health and diet.

To contact the author, visit
theinvisibleseed.com

Print Book 978-0-9966286-2-4

*In memory of my mother, Fatoumata L. Diallo,
who was and still is my greatest inspiration.*

Acknowledgements

I would like to thank my children: Assiatou Diallo, Aminata Diallo, Thierno Diallo, Mariama Barry, and Yaseen Barry. You were there every step of the way. You love me, encourage me, and believe in me. You truly push me forward. I love you all from the depths of my soul.

To my sisters: You kept pushing me, and you believed in my potential, even when I did not. I would not have gotten this far without your support. I love you, and I want to thank you from the bottom of my heart.

I would also like to thank: My family, friends, and the Institute of Integrative Nutrition and its community.

Also, I want to give a big thanks to my mentor and friend, Shavonne Morain. You are a beautiful human being, and you helped me to heal and to focus on the best parts of me.

To my Editor, Ayuba Fasasi, Thank you for your precious time and support.

To the team and clients at Diena Simply Natural, your love and support was my motivation.
Thank you.

Outline

A) Introduction
    I   My Story   1
    II "Bloo and the Invisible seed"   5
    III The Invisible seed   8
    IV The Balancing Tree   10

B) Mental and Spiritual Rebirth
    I   Happiness is a Choice   13
    II Personal Values   16
    III Relationships   20

C) Physical Rebirth
    I   Organization   24
        a) Organization and Goals   26
        b) Money Talks   27

    II Health & Wellness   29

    III Why I Quit Sugar   34

D) The Take Away   36

The Invisible Seed

My Story

When I was seven years old, my mother went away on a business trip. I visited a friend who lived/resided with her grandparents. They had a special hut outside for the children to play in. There was no door, but it was a very clean, inviting, and open area. This, especially, made it the ideal place to visit and play whenever my mom was away.

One day, my friend's grandmother cooked a very popular dish called 'futti'. (Ingredient: Bangladesh rice, okra, spinach, fermented spices, and palm oil.) It is a cheap and fast multidimensional meal with many different color and texture elements that satisfy any savory cravings. It was dinnertime, and the grandmother served all of us. We all ate happily, but 30 minutes later, I felt weird and sick. I soon fell asleep in the hut. When I woke up, it was the middle of the night and everyone was gone. On top of that, I had a burning fever and a heavy bladder. I realized I was in trouble, and I crawled outside to a mango tree. I was in a lot of pain, and I felt so alone. I did not want to die, and at that moment, the only thing I wanted was my mom next to me so she could hold and save me.

A sudden urge came over me, and I started talking to the tree and asking God to please bring my mom to me. I repeated it more than a hundred times before I fell asleep under the mango tree.

Around five in the morning, I woke up in my mother's arms. It was a miracle. She had come looking for me when she had gotten home and couldn't find me anywhere. She was crying and asked what had happened to me. I told her that it was the food that I ate. She gave me lots of water, and she kept reassuring me with her tender voice that I was going to be okay; and I believed her.

I took away four things that night. First, that day confirmed my faith in a higher power. Secondly, I realized my body can't tolerate certain types of food, and this was the first instance I recognized my bio individuality. Thirdly, since that day I've felt a deep connection to trees and Mother Nature. Lastly, a mother's love can heal and save.

Despite all of what happened that night, I still did not understand why I got sick. I often experienced similar symptoms anytime I was exposed to imported grains, sugar, and dairy. Back home I did okay because there was a huge variety of local foods, so I was able to avoid the foods that made me ill. However, when I moved from Guinea to the United States and was exposed to the American foods and diet, my health deteriorated with frequent outbreaks and sickness. This led to me taking a plethora of medication. I was dependent on the American medical care system for almost ten years. One day my doctor asked me what was wrong with me. I didn't know what to tell him. He referred me to a psychologist. Don't take me wrong. I've had some lifesaving treatments from some doctors, who were great listeners, but something had to give.

I opted out of seeing a psychologist. That was my breaking point. I decided to look outside the box for answers to my overwhelming health issues. After doing some research, I came across an article on gluten. I looked further into it, and I rejoiced. I lived a gluten and dairy free life for several years, after the fact, and I felt a bit better; but I was still having issues whenever I ate other grains and sugar.

I eventually quit sugar too, but the thing that really drove it home for me was the video lecture "Against the Grain: Chemical Genesis Mutation" by William Davis MD. He explained and gave proof backing the fact that most of the grains are genetically modified with high toxin chemicals in the U.S.A and shipped to certain places around the world, including Bangladesh.

Now, I can connect the dots and explain my first outbreak at age seven.

My health history is just one aspect of my life and my problems, as it is for many other people. What I learned from my experience is that it is never too late to start anew, change, heal, and grow. It took a lot of energy, healing, and owning my own power for me to rediscover and accept my limitless potential.

This book will show you the philosophy of the invisible seed as well as the physical tools I use to help me reach new heights in my life and health. My goal is to share it with you, so you can achieve it in your own personal life.

"Bloo and The Invisible Seed"

Growing up, my mother used to put me to bed with stories filled with life lessons and morals. These stories helped me to come to terms with some of the difficulties I dealt with. They gave me comfort when I felt alone. Now that I am older, and I have children of my own, I have passed most of these stories on to my children. The story of Bloo is an original story inspired by the invisible seed. All my children adore the story of Bloo, and I hope you do too.

"Bloo and The Invisible Seed"

Once upon a time, on a small farm at the edge of a riverbank, there lived a blue baby chick named Bloo. Soon after he hatched, Bloo found a seed in his shell. He would shove it between his feathers right over his heart for safekeeping. It filled him with such love and potential. He felt he could do anything as long as he had it with him. When all the other chicks saw him, however, his blue feathers frightened them.

"What is that?" They'd ask.

"It's not natural." They'd prod.

"Don't touch it, it might be contagious!" They'd poke.

All of this filled Bloo with pain and confusion. All he wanted to do was play and get on with his life but he was surrounded by negativity and fear. They taunted and ostracized him until one-day Bloo's seed disappeared and so did all of his hope.

He went to Mama Hen, and confided with her about his pain.

"THEY STOLE MY SEED!" He cried.

Now Mama Hen knew baby Bloo was different but she loved him regardless. She tucked him under her wing and whispered,

"Bloo, your seed was not stolen. You gave it away when you accepted all the bad things that were said to you. But, do not fret, for your seed is magic. As long as you remember the love and potential you felt on your first day of life, it will always come back to you."

All of a sudden baby Bloo was immersed in the love of Mama Hen. He remembered the feeling he felt on his first day of life and he made a decision in that moment. Regardless of how the other chicks treated him or what they said to him, he would never again give away his seed. He would always love and explore his potential. As he thought about this, the light in his heart grew, and he felt his seed tucked between his feathers right over his heart.

"Mama! It's back!" he embraced Mama Hen, rejoicing.

"See, it was never gone; it was just invisible"

The Invisible Seed

The invisible seed is the forgotten potential we all have within us. It is the potential we have to heal ourselves. To become whatever we dream and desire to become. It is the potential that we feel for a newborn baby. The misconception is that overwhelming potential diminishes over time. Well I've got news for you. It never disappeared. You just forgot about it. That is why it is important to remember it, acknowledge it, unlock it, and unleash it!

Since I was a child, my survival instinct pushed me to distinguish myself. It was a driving force inside of me that told me that I was worthy even though the world around me screamed that I was not. That invisible seed stuck with me through all the bad experiences, toxic relationships and illnesses until I unlocked it. When I finally acknowledged it, my life began to bloom.

When I acknowledged my worth and put it to the forefront of my life, I was able to overcome anxiety, fibromyalgia and panic attacks. I was able to go back to school to follow my dreams and to begin healing myself. I was reborn.

The key to change and healing begins with you acknowledging your invisible seed; the power you have within yourself to heal and flourish in life. You know you are worthy. Society and the world around you can dampen that feeling but the moment you acknowledge it, your seed is reborn.

The Balancing Tree

The balancing tree represents the essential elements for a balanced life. The roots (spirituality, knowledge, wellness, imagination, home organization) are the foundation of your life. Without these roots being healthy the tree above (profession, social connection, money, food, fitness, and relationships) would wither away.

The importance of maintaining a balanced tree of life is essential in order for you to achieve your bigger goals in life. Evaluate these basic elements in your life and start making adjustments and healthy changes that will nourish your tree and keep it balanced.

Sunshine = Acknowledgement
Water = Embracing
Love & Nurture = Research and implementing your self improvement/self care

Draw inspiration from every tree you see: You are a seed that has been planted in this world, and your job is to grow.

Personal growth equals; education, self-help resources; books, compact discs, etc. Listen and read spiritual and motivational materials in the morning and at night. Being resourceful, but more importantly learning from every situation or experience you encounter.

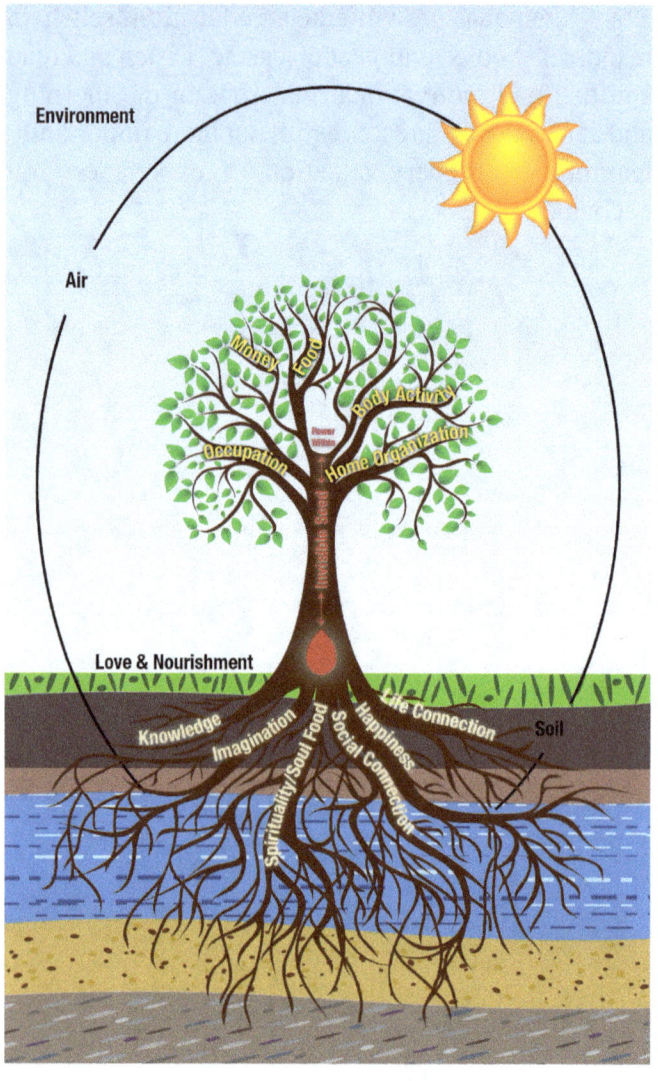

Happiness is a Choice

What is Happiness?

Full Definition of HAPPINESS
1 *obsolete* : good fortune : PROSPERITY
2 a : a state of well-being and contentment : JOY
   b : a pleasurable or satisfying experience
source: http://www.merriam-webster.com/dictionary/happiness

Working off this definition, I believe happiness is a state of mind in which you appreciate what you have and accept who you are despite the things you can't control. Happiness is learning to find a silver lining in all your problems and obstacles in life instead of just viewing them as a burden. You can approach your problems one of two ways: you can choose the bag filled with rocks or the bag filled with cotton balls. The choice is yours.

How to be positive in 4 Steps:

1) Breathing Exercises:

Breathe with your diaphragm. In through your nose, and out through your mouth and relax. By controlling your breathing, you will be able to keep control of your emotions and better assess your situation. This will help in allowing you to find the silver lining and to remain positive.

2) Reflect and Reevaluate:

This is where you step back and take an honest good look at your life. Become open to positive criticism and try to use it to improve yourself. Try and become more introspective about your life. This will allow you to look back and find correlations between your past and your present. Try to confront and overcome your emotional issues and burdens. This doesn't mean just getting over your issues, it means coming to terms with your past and choosing to not let it hold you back.

3) Let it go:

This means accepting the situation and deciding to release the stress of it from your life. Letting go is not the same as giving up, it is you accepting your situation for what it is and choosing to focus your energies on finding positive solutions.

4) Reaffirm:

You have made the decision to be positive, now you must keep reminding yourself of this decision. Look in the mirror every morning and promise yourself that you will maintain a positive outlook throughout your day. Go over the four steps as much as you feel you need to, and try to find your silver lining.

Personal Values

Your personal values are based on your life experiences. They build upon the values your parents and society instill in you as a child. As you grow older and have your own experiences, you make the decision on which of these values hold the most importance in your life.

Sometimes the values we learn as children are not always the most positive, but we hold the power to pick and choose what values we give power to within our lives. We have a responsibility to ourselves to reevaluate our values on a constant basis so that we can continue to grow. The more we understand about the values we hold dear, the more we can understand about ourselves.

One way to look at how our values are developed could be to see them as a tree. The invisible seed is the foundation of the tree. The tree you see above ground is not all there is, the roots of the tree expand just as far underground as the tree does above. The leaves grow towards the sun the roots stretch underground seeking water. Every part of the tree works towards finding what it needs so that it can become the magnificent tree it was meant to be. If these hidden parts of the tree were to wither and withdraw, the tree you see above ground would die as well. That is the balance.

You cannot grow unless you have your foot firmly planted on the ground. The key to being grounded is embracing your personal values, your uniqueness, your beliefs and your faith.

Core Values for Personal Growth

<u>Routines, Rituals, and Consistency</u> – The purpose of this is to get things done, to be stable, and to move forward and upward.

<u>Kindness & Compassion</u> – It is through love that we grow. Look at every being through the eyes of love.

<u>Humility </u>– "When you are humble you can learn"

<u>Honesty</u> – Living your own truth.

<u>Responsibility</u> – Accountability

<u>Trust</u> – Trust is having faith and going into the unknown. It is confronting fear.

<u>Respect</u> – Accepting and upholding every being or thing as they are.

<u>Gratitude</u> – Gratitude is having the attitude of thankfulness and looking at everything you have as a cherished gift.

<u>Uniqueness</u> – What is your authenticity? It comes

from the core values we described previously. Often times your gut is right. Authenticity is accepting the truths of your life, and embracing it. Being true to your feelings.

Beliefs – It is important to have some sort of spiritual beliefs or rituals. It feeds your soul. It is fundamental to know where you come from and to appreciate your culture, history, and background. It is also important to be open-minded to receiving and appreciating other cultures. This is necessary to make it possible for you to connect with other humans.

Seeking Knowledge – Accumulate knowledge and learn from yourself and from others. Learn from your mistakes and experiences. Study, read, ask questions, and experiment with new and different ideas and concepts.

Acceptance – Learn to accept people for who they are instead of trying to fix them into what you think they should be.

Relationships

Everyone has something special and unique to teach and to learn from one another. This means that every encounter should be treated as a valuable learning opportunity. A relationship is like the invisible seed. You plant it and nurture it so one day it will nourish you like a fruitful plant.

Always keep it simple. Internalize that old grade school saying, "Treat people the way you want to be treated". Be kind to the people around you and give your loved ones and friends' space without judgment.

Cultivate active listening, appreciation and recognition. Create a safety net for your loved ones and friends. Be present and celebrate accomplishments. Open your heart to receiving love. Communication is the fuel to maintain a healthy relationship. You can apply these principles to all the relationships in your life.

It is okay to be rejected. Rejection is a part of the growing cycle. Rejection is a learning opportunity. Accept the rejection, learn from it and move on because you can't please everyone.

You shouldn't go into relationships expecting the other person to understand you completely. Instead you should reverse your thinking and start relationships with an open mind and be willing to accept and understand the other person to the best of your ability. By starting relationships on this type of foundation, you will foster the positive relationships that you crave. People will be drawn to your positive and secure aura.

Being open to understanding others in a relationship does not however mean that you should allow yourself to get lost within the relationship. You should maintain an open and inviting approach to meeting new people but you should also be bold enough to be yourself.

Say what you want to say if it feels important to you. Don't allow yourself to be scared into submission because of a fear of rejection. Once you master this delicate balance of self-understanding, open mindedness, acceptance, and self-respect, you will find that your relationships will take on a healthier hue.

5 Helpful Hints To Communication

1) Maintain Steady Eye Contact
2) Practice Active Listening
3) Always Keep an Open Mind
4) Practice Being Humble
5) Practice Empathy

On the next page, I have set up an "Active Steps for Better Relationship" chart to help you actively resolve most of your relationship conflicts. You choose the person or object you have a relationship with. You identify the problems, conflicts, and/or improvements you'd like to address. You sit down with them to confront the conflict with this chart. It is important that both parties do this exercise together. Go over the "9 Mandatory Strategies for Communication" together. Then, apply them when conversing about your conflicts and come up with a solution together on how to resolve it. This chart is a guide you can use to bring most, if not all, of your relationships to a healthy level.

ACTIVE STEPS FOR BETTER RELATIONSHIPS

TYPE OF RELATIONSHIP

PROBLEMS, CONFLICTS, IMPROVEMENT

9 MANDATORY STRATEGIES FOR COMMUNICATION

RESULTS

PERSONAL
- Your own Body
- Mom or Dad
- Love Relationship
- Kids
- Relatives
- Friends
- Clients
- Co-Workers

LIFE
- Food
- Nature
- Pets

- Eye Contact
- Active Listening
- Respect
- Open Mind
- Acceptance
- Humility
- Gratitude
- Being Yourself
- Forgiveness

FOR EXAMPLE

Mom	Lack of Communication	Apply Strategies of Communication	We both sat down. We made eye contact and took turns asking about one another and our feelings. We were honest and respectful. We listened with open minds. I accepted her truth and she accepted mine. This was how we were able to forgive one another in the end. We showed gratitude for each other, because we loved one another for listening and being present for this exercise.

It is also important to remember there are positive and negative relationships. Sometimes you just need to clean the clutter from your life, and sometimes that's people. You know who or what they are. Fix what you can and let go of the rest.

Organization

Organization is a tool for achieving balance and reaching goals: Routines. Rituals. Consistency.

Step 1:
The first step is clearing out the clutter. Clean your home and office. Organize, rearrange, and decorate. Keep it simple and airy. This will help to clear your mind. Make it workable, efficient, and beautiful.

Step 2:
The second step is maintenance. This is an every moment sort of thing. This will be a ritual that you gain through constant repetition. Things such as: making your bed every morning; making cleaning or picking up after yourself an instant reaction to whatever you were doing; and making lists and itineraries.

Step 3:
The next step is to write down your goals and intentions. Get a calendar and post it up in your home. Make a schedule and put it on your calendar while incorporating a daily To-Do list to keep you organized. Update your schedule daily and make your To-Do list the night before.

Make sure you do something towards your short-term goals and your long-term goals every day. That is how you get things done. Know your priorities and get those done above all else. Then you can have room for other things.

GOAL CHART

Start now! Fill out this Goal Chart to get started!

HEALTH & WELL BEING	ACTION PLAN What skill or action you need to achieve your goals	TIME	FOCUS
10 YEARS ☐ ☐ ☐ ☐		↑	↑
5 YEARS ☐ ☐ ☐ ☐		↑	↑
2 YEARS ☐ ☐ ☐		↑	↑
1 YEAR ☐ ☐ ☐		↑	↑
6 MONTHS ☐ ☐ ☐		↑	↑
1 MONTH ☐ ☐ ☐		↑	↑
1 WEEK ☐ ☐ ☐		↑	↑
1 DAY ☐ ☐ ☐		↑	↑

MAKE SURE WHAT YOU DO EVERYDAY MOVES YOU TO YOUR BIGGEST GOAL!

Money Talks and Jigi et Jikke

We live in a society where money is fundamental to life. It is important to learn financial literacy because it is the key to money management.

My mother always told me how essential it was to save a portion of your income. She said bury it and forget it. Never spend it, and keep adding to it. The only time you dig it up is when you are adding to it.

Her words motivated me to always work hard to earn enough money to add to my buried treasure. I started saving at such a young age and as a result I have been able to stay financially afloat despite all that life has thrown my way. This is why I never worried about money.

The purpose of **Jigi** and **Jikke (Phonetic Pronunciation Jeegee and Jeekkeh) is to create a mental state where you are always aw**are of your ability to be more productive. Don't allow yourself to be content with the bare minimum. Don't allow yourself to settle. **Jigi and Jikke** is constantly reminding you to find opportunities to maintain a financial safety net.

MONEY BUDGETING

of your INCOME

50% is spent on your needs: housing, transportation, food, childcare, insurance and mandatory debt pay-down.

5% Jigi Jikke* or abundance of money. The money you never touch.

15% Savings

30% is spent on wants, things that make you happy.

❖ ❖ ❖ ❖ ❖

If you look at your current income situation, and you find that you are living paycheck to paycheck. Maybe it is time to look for a new skill or business opportunity. Even with children or sickness, there is a way. We are all entrepreneurs, and the limits in that field are boundless. You just need to have vision and to look hard enough. Have a vision, believe in it, and take action. Where there is a will, there is always away.

Health & Wellness/ Self-Care & Nutrition

Self-Care:
Taking care of yourself is essential for your wellbeing. What does it mean to take care of your self? It isn't just buying fancy clothes and wearing nice makeup. Self-Care is the act of loving your self - body and soul. It is treating your body like your temple. You must take time out in your life to maintain the small little details that you normally overlook about yourself.

• Nurturing your spirituality:
Open your heart to spirituality. You don't have to conform to any specific belief system, but you should try and find something that brings your peace and fills that spiritual void that may need nourishing. Having a personal relationship with a divine power has brought me an unparalleled amount of comfort and balance in my journey through life. No matter what got thrown my way or what obstacles I had to face, my faith has given me the strength I needed to keep going strong.

• Taking care of your physical health:

It is hard to be an active member of society if you are always lacking in energy, are sick, or are just unhappy with your physical health and appearance. Exercise plays an essential role in our health. Studies have shown that constant physical activity strengthens your muscles, improves your cardiovascular functions, releases endorphins that promote positive emotions, reduces the risks of obesity, increases libido and stamina, and promotes longevity. I have noticed that after an exercise session, I am happier, more energetic, and better focused. By adding at least thirty minutes of exercise into your routine, every day, you could improve your quality of life.

• Treat Yourself:

You treat yourself because you love yourself. You work hard every day trying to take care of your responsibilities and the people in your life, but it is important not to forget about yourself. It is fundamental that you realize that you are a priority in life. Take time out every day to pamper yourself because you earned it.

If you've worked hard all month, then you deserve to splurge on whatever it is that makes you happy. This could be a massage, a day off at the park, going to a concert, getting your hair done, or anything: as long as it makes you happy. Make sure to make time out to do these things.

• Restful Sleep: In our society there is a pandemic of sleep deprivation. It is our responsibility to respect and make time for sleep. Sleep is fundamental for our bodies to heal and recuperate. The reality is that our sleep pattern affects us both mentally and physically. If you're not getting your eight hours of restful sleep, you need to take steps to correct that. You can try adding exercise to your routine, eating more nutritious food, and meditation. If all these things don't work, see a doctor.

• Food & Nutrition: Why is it important to eat clean and organic foods versus conventional foods? It's better for you because whole foods are nutritious. Your body needs these whole and nutritious foods to help it to grow, thrive, and heal itself.

Conventional food is full of pesticides, chemicals and GMO's (Genetically Modified Food) that can destroy you at a cellular level. Listen to your body. Most of the time your body will manifest physical reactions to foods that are not good for you: A headache, stomachache, bloating, hair loss, sluggishness, and even breakouts. Listen to your body and eliminate the foods in your diet that your body rejects.

Treat your body as a temple and your best friend. Give it more attention, love, respect, gratitude, and especially the right food. Healthy cooking is a great way to stay away from high processed foods and save money. It is also a great way to experiment with new food in the kitchen. A good home-cooked meal has been known to bring people together, especially when it is made with love.

• Food Preparation:

A great way to keep your life organized is by preparing all your meals for the week ahead of time. If you dedicate a day in the week to get all your shopping and cooking done, it will allow you to spend the rest of your week towards achieving your goals. Even if you are not preparing every meal, you can do the grunt work such as: Chopping up fruits and vegetables, baking or cooking your starches, and preparing your sauces all in bulk so it will last through your week.

• Fashion - Reinventing your Style:

The golden rule: The way you present yourself on the outside should reflect how you see yourself on the inside. Dressing well is not a matter of vanity, but a matter of self-upkeep. The way you choose to present yourself on the outside is your calling card. Dress for your ambitions and success, and before you know it, you will be there.

Health Tip: Avoid wearing synthetic clothing and chemically processed cosmetics. Wear natural fibers such as cotton, and for cosmetics look for herb and mineral based products.

Why I Quit Sugar

Sugar was literally killing me. It has been proven that sugar causes cystic candidiasis and inflammation which leads to all kinds of diseases, such as: acid reflux, indigestion, constipation, skin disease, eczema, scalp and hair disorders, overgrown candidiasis, depression, high blood pressure, diabetes, obesity, cancer and many more. It is also a scientific fact that sugar is eight times more addictive than many illegal drugs. Visit bodyecology.com to gain links to further research articles about the subject.

By quitting sugar, I lost 30 pounds and I managed to overcome inflammation, kidney stones, water retention, breakouts, dandruff, hair loss, chronic fatigue, fibromyalgia, headaches, parathyroid disorder, acid reflux, anxiety, bloating, and panic attacks.

In order to quit sugar, I basically added more green vegetables, fruits, and liquids to my diet. I did a three day jump-start fast of my own creation and supplemented it with natural herbs and vitamins. I maintained my sugar free lifestyle with careful planning and the help from holistic health coaching.

I encourage all my readers to look into finding a health coach to better their lives through food and nutrition.

The Take Away

The Invisible seed is a symbol of our hope. The invisible seed represents the power we possess to constantly grow and change. It represents the fact that it is never too late to start over, go further, or be happier. The seed is only invisible because we have lost faith in its existence, so we have to continuously remind ourselves that it exists. Remind our selves of our infinite potential. I know this! You know this! So let us own it and use it to achieve our dreams!

This book is not just a reminder; it is a tool to help get you started. These tools will always be here. So when you find yourself fallen or distressed, you can always come back to these tools to put you back on the right track and to propel you forward.

The time is now! It is always now! Life is unpredictable, but you have the power to control your mind and your body. This is a feat that takes many a lifetime to achieve. It takes focus, discipline and commitment. Yet the tools such as the charts and the balancing tree will give you an advantage in your quest to achieve your goals. Use the balancing tree to balance your life so you can go achieve your dreams with absolute conviction!

* Fun exercise:

Let's plant a tree. I want us all to pay homage to the trees that this book has continually alluded to. As a symbol of your new beginning, I implore you to plant a new tree or as many as you wish. It will be a symbol of your journey and you can watch this tree grow throughout the upcoming years. It will be a motivation and a reminder of your invisible seed and the little balancing tree in your life. It will be a symbol of gratitude and compassion. This is how we can give back.

Thank you & May the Invisible Seed be with you!
Diena Diallo

www.ingramcontent.com/pod-product-compliance
Lightning Source LLC
Chambersburg PA
CBHW052132010526
44113CB00034B/1894